Dinosaurs

Jozua Douglas & Barbara van Rheenen

Clavis
NEW YORK

Have you ever seen a dinosaur in your backyard?
Probably not. All dinosaurs are long gone.
Dinosaurs lived a very, very, very long time ago.
Come on, we'll go on a trip to the past.
Let's go looking for dinosaurs!

In the time of dinosaurs the world looked entirely different than it does today. There was no grass. And there were no flowers. There were no dogs, cats, or chickens. There weren't even any humans. There were a lot of other animals around that don't exist anymore today, though.

What is a Dinosaur?

Back then, there were lots of types of dinosaurs. Some were gigantic, others were very small. Most dinosaurs lived on land and laid eggs. Most dinosaurs had thick, scaly skin. Do you know an animal that looks like a dinosaur? An elephant is indeed very big. But an elephant doesn't lay eggs. Dinosaurs actually looked most like reptiles such as crocodiles and lizards, which have scaly skin and lay eggs.

Did you know in the time of the dinosaurs there were crocodiles? You also could find spiders, dragonflies, turtles, and fish.

Some flying creatures could grow as big as a small airplane!

Besides dinosaurs, there were lots of other big and small creatures who lived in the water and flew in the sky.

The marine creature **Liopleurodon** had a mouth that was nearly seven feet long!

Did you know there were miniature dinosaurs? Some were as small as a chicken!

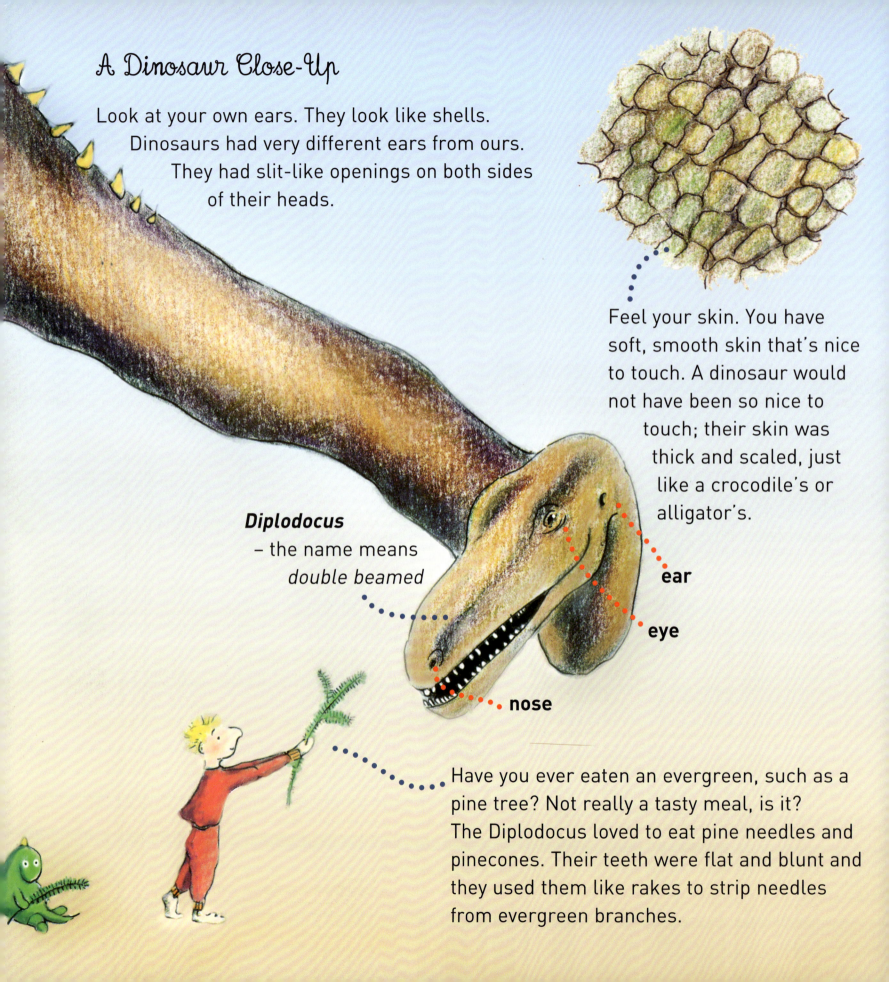

A Dinosaur Close-Up

Look at your own ears. They look like shells. Dinosaurs had very different ears from ours. They had slit-like openings on both sides of their heads.

Feel your skin. You have soft, smooth skin that's nice to touch. A dinosaur would not have been so nice to touch; their skin was thick and scaled, just like a crocodile's or alligator's.

Diplodocus – the name means *double beamed*

ear
eye
nose

Have you ever eaten an evergreen, such as a pine tree? Not really a tasty meal, is it? The Diplodocus loved to eat pine needles and pinecones. Their teeth were flat and blunt and they used them like rakes to strip needles from evergreen branches.

Tyrannosaurus Rex – the name means *king of the tyrant lizards*

Did you know some dinosaurs had feathers?

The **teeth** of the Tyrannosaurus Rex were extremely sharp and often up to 9 inches long! They ripped and tore big pieces of meat with their teeth and had huge mouths. How much do you think could fit in there?

Herbivores (Plant-Eaters)

Plant-eating longneck dinosaurs are the biggest land animals that ever existed. They could grow as tall as eighty-five feet—that's as tall as two upright school buses on top of each other! Such creatures could weigh more than ten elephants—that's more than eighty tons or 160,000 pounds! At that time there weren't any trees with leaves, but there were a lot of *coniferous* trees—trees with needles and cones. You also could find ferns, palms, and plants that we call "horsetails." Plant-eating dinosaurs loved them.

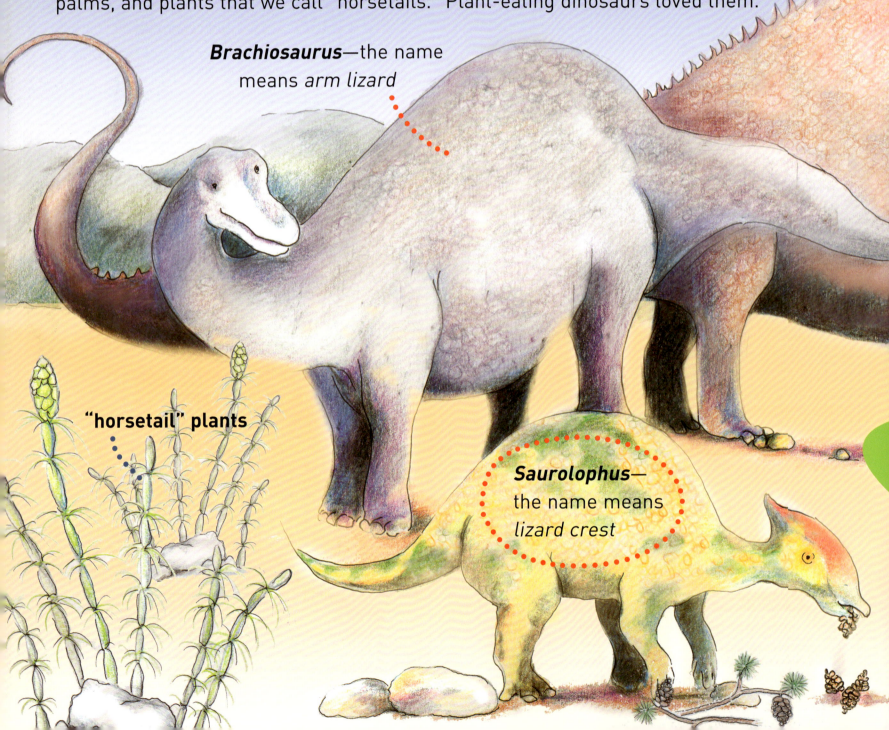

Brachiosaurus—the name means *arm lizard*

"horsetail" plants

Saurolophus—the name means *lizard crest*

The plant-eating longneck dinosaurs probably ate all day long. They needed food to fill their gigantic bodies. Imagine cooking those big creatures a meal! You would need pots and pans as big as trucks! And how much dung would those giant dinosaurs produce every day, do you think?

Diplodocus—the name means *double beamed*

Did you know some dinosaurs had beaks?

Did you know ts of dinosaurs ate rocks? Digesting rocks helped to crush food in their stomachs.

Triceratops— the names means *head with three horns*

Velociraptor—the name means *fast robber*

Raptors could probably run very fast.
They had huge, sharp claws.
We think they hunted in groups.

Dinosaur Dave

1.
I DREAMED I FOUND A HUGE EGG IN MY BACKYARD.

2.
I DRAGGED IT HOME AND NESTLED IT IN MY BED.

3.
SOON, THE EGG STARTED TO CRACK. AND THEN A DINOSAUR HATCHED! "MOM," I CALLED. "THERE'S A DINOSAUR IN MY ROOM!"

4.
"CAN I KEEP IT?" I ASKED. MY MOTHER THOUGHT FOR A WHILE. "WHO WILL FEED HIM? WHO WILL WALK HIM?" "ME!" I YELLED. "ME, ME, ME!"

5.
"WELL, ALL RIGHT THEN," MOM SAID. DADDY BUILT A HOUSE FOR IT.

6.
I CALLED IT DAVE. I CUT HIM SOME BRANCHES FROM OUR PINE TREE.

7.
DAVE ATE ALL OF THE BRANCHES. HE ATE AND ATE AND ATE. HE WANTED MORE AND MORE.

8. AND THEN DAVE STARTED GROWING. HE GREW AND GREW AND GREW UNTIL HE WAS BIGGER THAN OUR HOUSE!

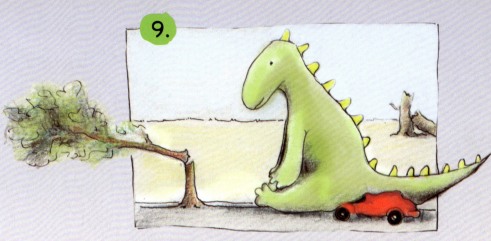

9. DAVE DRANK UP THE ENTIRE POND. HE KNOCKED OVER TREES. AND THEN HE SAT DOWN, RIGHT ON OUR CAR! "WILL YOU PLEASE WALK HIM NOW?" MY MOTHER ASKED.

10. I WALKED DOWN THE STREET WITH DAVE. HE ATE UP ALL THE LITTLE TREES AND PEED IN OUR NEIGHBOR'S YARD. THEN HE POOPED IN THE STREET.

11. A POLICE OFFICER CAME ALONG. HE LOOKED ANGRY. "ARE YOU GOING TO CLEAN UP THIS MESS?"

12. LUCKILY, THAT WAS WHEN I WOKE UP. I THINK I'LL ASK FOR A DOG FOR MY BIRTHDAY.

Do you like to make noise? Parasaurolophus was probably the biggest noise-maker of all. It had a huge crest on its head. Was it a snorkel? Or was it a horn with which the dinosaur could warn others whenever danger was near?

Parasaurolophus—the name means *crested lizard*.

Pachycephalosaurus *(thick-headed lizard)* probably fought by bumping their thick domed heads together.

Triceratops *(three-horned face)* had three sharp horns with which it protected itself.

Dinosaur Babies

When dinosaur babies hatched, they were quite small. You could put a dinosaur hatchling right on your lap. After that, though, dinosaurs grew very fast. Do you think dinosaur babies had lots of friends?

Did you know dinosaur babies had a special sharp tooth to break their eggs all by themselves?

This is a dinosaur egg. It would have been about as big as a page of this book!

Dinosaurs made nests for their eggs on the ground with sand and pine needles. Dinosaurs laid many eggs at once and hatched as many as twenty babies at one time.

Dinosaur Mysteries

No human has ever seen a dinosaur. That is why we know so little about them.
How do you think a dinosaur slept? Lying down? Or standing up?
Would they have snored? We don't know what sounds they made.
Would the tough Tyrannosaurus Rex have roared? Or did it make soft peeping sounds?
Did the huge Diplodocus let out loud farts? What do you think?

Nobody knows exactly what color dinosaurs were. What do you think? Were there purple dinosaurs? Or dinosaurs with spots and stripes? Most dinosaurs were probably gray or green. That way, they could blend in with their surroundings, which would have been safer for them.

These questions are all mysteries.
Maybe you'll want to study dinosaurs and become a dinosaur investigator.
Then you can figure all of this out for us.

Maybe they sometimes did, like elephants do. ...nosaur, you can easily walk through the water.

Did you know Stegosaurus was as big as a pick-up truck and its brain was as small as a walnut?

We don't know if land dinosaurs could swim. Of course when you're as tall as a longneck d

Ankylosaurus *(fused lizard)* was built like a tank. It had a kind of armor with spines on its back and its tail ended in a dangerous club made of bone.

Stegosaurus *(covered or roof lizard)* had plates along its back and sharp spikes on its tail.

The Dinosaur Investigator

The dinosaur investigator looks for dinosaur tracks. Today he's very happy for he's uncovered the skeleton of a Diplodocus. Very carefully, the investigator chips away the skeleton from the sandy stone. It takes a while to do this. A photographer takes pictures of the bones, so everyone will know exactly how they were positioned in the ground.

What is the Dinosaur Investigator Looking For?
A dinosaur investigator doesn't only look for dinosaur bones. He also looks for fossils of dinosaur dung, dinosaur eggs, and dinosaur tracks. These fossils are as rock-hard as the bones because they turned into stone over many, many years.
The dung tells the investigator what the dinosaurs used to eat. The tracks tell him how dinosaurs used to walk and how fast they could go. The eggs tell the investigator where the dinosaurs used to build their nests.

What Does the Dinosaur Investigator Need?

Do you want to dig up a dinosaur? Then you'll need a lot of things. The dinosaur investigator uses shovels, hammers, chisels, fine brushes, gloves, a helmet, protective goggles, tape measures, and bone glue. The glue is to fix bones that are broken or accidently get broken.

Did you know a dinosaur investigator sometimes uses a toothbrush to clean bones?

The Museum

Do you want to see for yourself how tall a dinosaur was? Then you have to go on a dinosaur hunt in a dinosaur museum. They have a lot of dinosaur skeletons there. Stand next to the skeletons to see how awe-inspiringly huge these creatures really were.

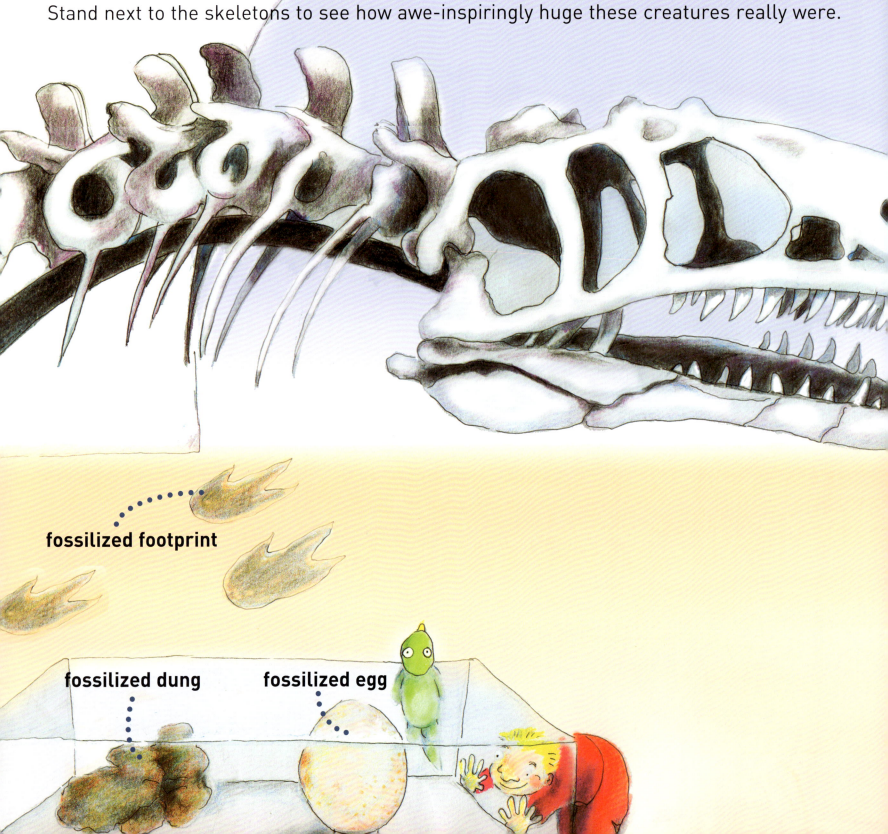

fossilized footprint

fossilized dung

fossilized egg

Did you know over 1,000 types of dinosaurs have been found?

Big Dinosaur's Rumbling Belly

Big dinosaur's rumbling belly—
He was so hungry. He was so hungry.
Big dinosaur's rumbling belly—
He hid inside a great big bush.

Little dinosaur—*clip-clop, clip-clop*.
He was daydreaming. He was daydreaming.
Little dinosaur—*clip-clop, clip-clop*.
He wasn't watching and then: *Gobble, gobble, gulp!*

Dinosaur Hunt

It is dark and it is night.
Let's go and hunt for dinosaurs.
We stalk through the dinosaur woods.
Look out, look out, they're running free!

Let's go and hunt for dinosaurs.
We stalk, crawl, whisper softly.
Look out, there's a big one
with a huge tail and claws!

Let's go and hunt for dinosaurs.
We run through the dinosaur woods.
We'll just look for a small one—
just a little, bitty baby one!

Dinosaur Finger Puppets

You will need:

   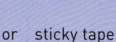

scissors   (colored) paper   glue   or   sticky tape   pencil

1. Draw the profile of a dinosaur head twice. Draw eyes and teeth on it or make one with a big horn! If you use a white piece of paper, you can color it in yourself.

2. Cut a strip of paper about as big as half of your middle finger. Then wrap it around your finger and stick it together with glue or tape (not too tightly!). You've made a small tube.

3. Stick the dinosaur profiles to the top of the paper tube.

4. In the same way as you made the tube, make four smaller tubes for the feet. These will fit around your thumb, forefinger, ring finger, and pinkie.

5. Now you have your own dinosaur!

Dino-Quiz

1. What reptile that exists today was also alive in the time of the dinosaurs?

2. Who was the king of the dinosaurs?

3. What kind of ears did dinosaurs have?

4. Which dinosaurs were the biggest that ever existed?

5. How small was the miniature dinosaur?

6. What did longneck dinosaurs eat?

7. What did Tyrannosaurus Rex eat?

8. How big was the biggest dinosaur egg?

9. Why does the dinosaur investigator look for dinosaur dung?

10. How does the dinosaur investigator clean skeleton bones?

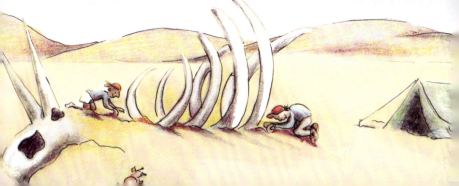

Answers

1. Crocodile.

2. Tyrannosaurus Rex.

3. Slit-like openings on both sides of their heads.

4. Plant-eating longneck dinosaurs.

5. As small as a chicken.

6. Plants, pine needles, and pinecones.

7. Smaller dinosaurs.

8. As big as a page of this book.

9. To determine what dinosaurs ate.

10. With brushes—sometimes a toothbrush.

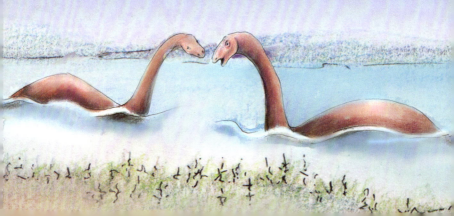

Dinosaur Feet!

To which dinosaur do these feet belong?

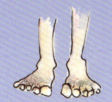
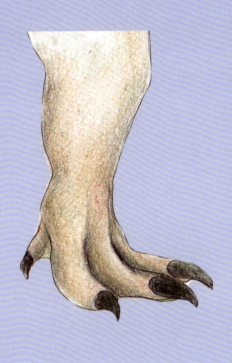